*This Journal Belongs to:*

______________________________

# YOU ARE HOME

## GUIDED JOURNAL

***A Transformative Journey Toward Radical Self-Love***

TARN ELLIS

MANDALA

SAN RAFAEL LOS ANGELES LONDON

## About the

# YOU ARE HOME

## GUIDED JOURNAL

This journal is a tool to help you cultivate self-love. Allow it to take you on a journey of discovery as you reflect on the past, consider the present, and look toward the future. Each section covers an important self-love topic, such as gratitude, positivity, body image, or abundance, all of which have been curated to help you love yourself better.

This journal gives you permission to feel good about being *you*. It asks you to change nothing about yourself except your mindset, reminding you that you are perfect exactly as you are. Inside these pages, you will find uplifting art, thought-provoking writing prompts, and mindful affirmations. This journal will help you think more positively, live more authentically, and most importantly, show yourself more love and appreciation!

# How to Use This Journal

The *You Are Home Guided Journal* contains 15 sections. Each section addresses a different subject related to self-love. Although it's totally up to you how to complete your journal, here's what we recommend.

Start at the beginning, in the section titled, "The Past." Plan to work through one section per week. At the beginning of each week, look through the artwork and affirmations for that section. Think about how they make you feel and what they mean to you. When you're ready, start working through the prompts for that section. Take your time. The number of prompts varies from section to section, and some prompts may feel harder to answer than others. Spend as long as you need on each prompt. You can also skip a prompt and come back to it after responding to the rest of the prompts for that section. But do try to complete the whole section by the end of each week so you're ready for the next section the following week.

Working through your journal this way will help you cultivate a deep sense of self-love. By the time you reach the end, you will have discovered which parts of yourself feel the most difficult to love and will have started down the path toward *truly* loving them.

# THE PAST

# What is your favorite childhood memory?

I learn and grow from my experiences.

I forgive myself for
my past mistakes.

What is a mistake you made in the past that taught you a valuable lesson?

Write a letter to your childhood self, showing love and understanding.

Dear little me...

I let go of what
no longer serves me.

Allow yourself to acknowledge how far you've come as you reflect on the past year. What changes have you made, and how have you grown?

What is something you've been holding on to that you can let go of now?

I am at peace
with my past.

# SELF-WORTH

Write a love letter to yourself.

Dear me...

I am
worthy.

What qualities do you love most about yourself?

# What are you most proud of?

I am complete. I am whole.
I am enough.

I love and appreciate myself.

# What are you really good at?

# INNER PEACE

I have a place of
peace within myself.

# I feel most peaceful when . . .

What does "safe haven" mean to you?

I am filled with calm energy, able to feel tranquil and serene whenever I choose.

I choose not to worry about things outside of my control.

Write a list of things outside of your control that you don't need to worry about.

How do you protect your inner peace, and how can you bring more peace into your life moving forward?

Calmness washes over me with every deep breath.

# POSITIVITY

I choose to replace my negative thoughts with positive, loving ones.

How can you take one of your perceived problems or challenges and look on the bright side of it?

Write a list of all the wonderful things in your life.

I see every mistake and hardship as a valuable lesson.

I approach each day with hope and positivity.

How can you begin this day in the most positive and optimistic way?

# PRESENT

# During which activities do you feel the most present?

I pay attention to the present moment.

I am exactly where I am supposed to be.

What can you change in your daily life to help stay more in the moment?

# How would you sum up your life right now?

I can use my breath to feel
grounded and present.

# EMPOWERMENT

What have you achieved that used to be a dream for the future?

I have the power to change my story.

I am in control of my life.

Write a list of all the things within your control.

# What aspects of your life do you take pride in?

I am creating the life I have always dreamed of.

I can overcome any challenges that life throws at me.

# What recent achievements, actions, or growth are you proud of?

# SELF-CONFIDENCE

# When do you feel the most confident?

I am filled with self-confidence.

I believe in myself.

# When do you doubt yourself?

Write a list of reasons you should believe in yourself and be proud of yourself.

I am proud
to be me.

# INTUITION

I listen to my inner voice.

When did you have a gut instinct about something or someone that turned out to be right?

How does it feel when your intuition is trying to speak to you?

I tune in to my intuition
and let it guide me.

I trust my own wisdom.

Tuning in to your intuition, what guidance does it offer on a current decision you need to make?

# REST

What activities do you enjoy that help you relax and unwind?

I allow myself to rest,
knowing I have done enough.

It's fine to do nothing.

Do you put too much pressure on yourself to be productive? If so, how?

How can you make more time for rest in your life?

Rest and relaxation
are necessary.

# PLAY

I am playful and fun-loving.

# Write a list of things you do for fun.

What is the best adventure you've been on?

I enjoy the lightness
of living.

I honor my inner child by prioritizing play and adventure.

# What do you take too seriously?

# GRATITUDE

# What are the five things that you are most grateful for?

1. 

2. 

3. 

4. 

5. 

I appreciate the beauty of the world around me.

I am grateful for all of life's blessings.

# What brings you joy on a daily basis?

Who in your life do you appreciate and why?

I find beauty in small things.

# BODY IMAGE

# What do you love most about your body?

I love my body and all that it does for me.

My body is fit, strong,
and healthy.

# How can you show your body more love and care?

What joyful activities do you pursue that are good for your body and soul?

I am beautiful, inside and out.

## Write a love letter to your body.

Dear body, thank you for...

# ABUNDANCE

Prosperity and success flow to me.

In what areas of your life do you feel the most abundant?

In what areas of your life do you feel scarcity or a lack?

Abundance is a mindset.

How can you change the way you view scarcity or lack to attract more abundance?

I have an abundance of
happiness in my life.

Write a list of the hopeful, positive, joyful things you believe about the world.

# VULNERABILITY

I return to my wildest, purest, most authentic self.

When have you opened up to someone about something that felt raw and vulnerable?

Is fear of judgment or shame holding you back from saying or expressing anything?

I allow myself to be vulnerable with others.

I have the courage to speak my truth.

What would you tell the world if you had the courage to do so?

# THE FUTURE

I am actively creating the future I've always imagined.

# What are you looking forward to in the near future?

# MY VISION BOARD

Use this space to draw all the things you would like in your future.

Where would you like to be five years from now?

I am hopeful for a wonderful future.

I keep my heart and mind open to the opportunities life presents.

# What qualities do you want your future self to have?

Write out your action plan to achieve your dreams.

I am manifesting my dreams.

MANDALA

An imprint of MandalaEarth
PO Box 3088
San Rafael, CA 94912
www.MandalaEarth.com

Find us on Facebook: www.facebook.com/MandalaEarth

**Publisher** Raoul Goff
**VP Publishing** Roger Shaw
**Publishing Director** Katie Killebrew
**Editor** Peter Adrian Behravesh
**Editorial Assistant** Amanda Nelson
**VP Creative Director** Chrissy Kwasnik
**Art Director** Ashley Quackenbush
**Senior Designer** Stephanie Odeh
**VP Manufacturing** Alix Nicholaeff
**Production Associate** Tiffani Patterson
**Senior Production Manager, Subsidiary Rights** Lina s Palma-Temena

MandalaEarth would also like to thank Jessica Easto.



ISBN: 979-8-88762-108-1

Manufactured in China by Insight Editions
10 9 8 7 6 5 4 3 2 1

ROOTS of PEACE REPLANTED PAPER

Insight Editions, in association with Roots of Peace, will plant two trees for each tree used in the manufacturing of this book. Roots of Peace is an internationally renowned humanitarian organization dedicated to eradicating land mines worldwide and converting war-torn lands into productive farms and wildlife habitats. Roots of Peace will plant two million fruit and nut trees in Afghanistan and provide farmers there with the skills and support necessary for sustainable land use.